THE HEROES IN OUR CLASSROOMS

IN OUR

CLASSROOMS

UNFORGETTABLE STORIES FROM TEACHERS WHO BELIEVE IN THE POWER OF EDUCATION

CHERI DIXON ALONG WITH 7 OTHER
INSPIRATIONAL EDUCATORS

Table of Contents

INTRODUCTION

Cheri Dixon Consulting was created after I stepped away from a very successful career in public education. I served different communities during my 28 years as a teacher and principal, working to improve schools that needed some extra love and support. I began to realize that I still had so many goals and dreams to accomplish in my life, so stepping into the world of entrepreneurship allowed me to do just that and I opened my business in June of 2023.

I believe in the power of a teacher. Ask anyone and their most memorable childhood experiences are usually connected to their school or teacher interactions. Teachers not only educate the future but influence their students' future paths by providing love and support.

As I build and expand Cheri Dixon Consulting, I know supporting teachers and schools will continue to be a priority. The Heroes in Our Classrooms is just one step in my journey that lies ahead.

The Heroes in Our Classrooms

Unforgettable Stories from Teachers Who Believe in the Power of Public Education

Everyone hears the stories of how challenging teaching can be. The pay is not at the same level as other professions. The mandates can be daunting. And teachers never work just a 9-5 job. They live, eat, and breathe ways to continually improve their students' chances of understanding all of the required curriculum day in and day out.

This has caused quite a disruption to the profession. Great teachers are not only retiring, but simply leaving due to stress and overwhelm. College students are veering away from entering the profession all together. And we all know that students need a teacher in the classroom teaching them, forcing administrators to hire unqualified candidates, in hopes that they can build their skills quickly and ensure student success.

How do we keep our great teachers coming back each year? How do we encourage our young adults to choose their path in education? These may not be questions we can answer today, but this book is our attempt to share our own personal stories of why we chose our career path and nuggets of wisdom that may make the journey for others just as fulfilling.

I chose this team to partner with me on this journey, as each of them (along with so many others) has truly had an impact on my own educational career. Each story brings a different perspective in hopes anyone out there in the thick of it, or dreaming of teaching children, can resonate and understand the awesomeness of this profession.

We don't do it for the money.
We don't do it for the fame.
We do it because it is a calling…the hardest job you will ever love!

Thank you to everyone who made this project possible. She Rises Studios who always support us with our big ideas and help us make these projects a reality. My own teachers, who inspired me to join the profession. My colleagues and mentors on my journey. My supervisors, who trusted me to do what I knew needed to be done to grow students and teachers to be their best. My friends and family, who allowed me to share my stories of success, and let me cry on those tough days that come along. My daughter, who served as my guinea pig, as I developed and tried new strategies along my journey. My former assistant principals, who helped me rebuild each of the schools that I led.

And a special thank you to my co-authors who said yes when I proposed this project. You all truly inspire me, and so many others. You have made a huge impact on the world, and I am proud to not only have you on this team, but to have you by my side on my own journey as a teacher!

Cheri Dixon

Cheri Dixon

Founder of Cheri Dixon Consulting, LLC

https://www.linkedin.com/in/cheri-dixon-38938b244/
https://www.facebook.com/cheri.dixon.35
https://www.instagram.com/cheridixonconsulting/
https://www.cheridixonconsulting.com

Cheri Dixon is the owner of Cheri Dixon Consulting LLC, which she started after leaving a 28-year career in public education. Cheri lives in Houston and now takes her work into the business world, helping businesses scale their organizations to the next level. Cheri believes that the leader is crucial to success and supports leaders to develop their skills to strive for excellence in this global society. Cheri is an international best-selling author, podcast host, and has an award-winning talk show. Cheri loves spending time with her daughter, her chocolate lab-pitbull, and running her yearly half marathon!

EVERY CHILD DESERVES A CHAMPION

By Cheri Dixon

"Every child deserves a champion: an adult who will never give up on them, who understands the power of connection and insists they become the best they can possibly be." —Rita Pierson

I began my teaching career in 1995, and I was blessed to have had the opportunity to hear Rita Pierson speak during one of my first convocations in my district. I began my career in a diverse district on the east side of Houston, Texas, and many of our students came to us at school to be loved and cared for. Hearing Rita Pierson speak about her experiences, her mother's experiences (also as a teacher), and the tremendous progress her students made each year all because she cared for them, loved them, pushed them, and made them believe they could be anything they wanted, no matter their circumstances. This resonated with me the moment I heard it. As a matter of fact, I remember thinking at that very moment, "I will not give up on any of my students. I will get them on a path of success....no matter how difficult it may be."

That convocation took place in the late 1990s; however, I found my desire to teach at the young age of six years old…in 1977. I know, no one determines their lifelong career at six years old. Well, no one but me. I owe that life-changing decision to my first-grade teacher. She was amazing, and I remember thinking how lucky I was that she chose me to be in her class (yes, at the age of six I believed that the teachers chose their students each year…almost like an NFL draft session). But it wasn't only because she kept us engaged in the learning but also provided us with the right level of support that pushed us while not overwhelming us as we learned how to read. You see, I had two working parents, and my mom would tend to get a bit distracted and overwhelmed back then. She would sometimes forget to pick me up at the end of the day. If you have ever been left behind when all of the other students went home, left to be alone in the front office while they tried to locate your mom, wondering if there was an accident or something horrific happening because you were sure that would be the only reason she would forget about you…well, then you understand how significant it was when my teacher refused to leave me there to wait alone. No, she brought me back to her room and gave me the greatest gift anyone could have given…she let me help her prepare for the next school day!

I will never forget it! I erased the chalkboard. I stapled papers. I passed out the needed materials. And I have to say, I know I was her best helper ever! There were even times she let me WRITE on that chalkboard! And to be honest, I know that was the moment that I believed I would become a teacher. It sounds silly, right? But here is what that experience did for me. It taught me that my teacher cared. It made me believe I wasn't someone who was left behind. And of course, as we worked together, we had conversations where she shared with me that she believed I would do big things in my life one day. I was ready…sign me up for an education course in college and let me be the superhero to others that she was for me!

As I continued in my own educational experiences growing up, this was a pattern. Teachers understood the different struggles I was experiencing, understood my drive to do amazing things in life, and understood my need to be reassured that I could accomplish all my goals. As a matter of fact, one of my co-authors in this book was one of those superheroes to me many years ago! I left high school, ready for college, knowing that I was entering a profession that mattered. One that made a difference in the world. And I knew then that I would do whatever it took to not only get into that classroom, but also to prepare my students, love my students, and build their belief in themselves so that they too could believe that anything in life, no matter your circumstances, is possible!

Teaching is not an easy task. If you are a teacher reading this, you get it! If you are a former teacher, this was your every day! If you are a future educator, get ready! Not only was college a bit overwhelming (well, I did become a teenage mother, and that brought a whole other set of challenges in my path), but then I took my first teaching job 1,000 miles from my hometown without any support from my family. I walked into that first classroom with so many mixed emotions…excitement to begin my career but also overwhelmed as I was placed in the farthest portable building from the school entrance. I had to figure out what to do next on my own! That first year was a doozy, and honestly, I planned to quit at the end of the first semester. Nothing about that first part of the year was anything like my dream! I wondered every day how my teachers made this job look so glamorous, so fulfilling, when I was going home each day in tears. The struggle was real!

But it turns out, I am not a quitter. During my Christmas break, I discussed all my struggles with my then-husband and realized that maybe because of the stress and overwhelm of not only starting a new career but also moving across the country, I was making a rash decision and that I would stick it out until the end of the year. However, I was determined to leave in May, move back to my small town, and open a daycare. I justified spending tens of thousands of dollars on my college education with the fact that I would be the BEST daycare owner ever! And, as they say…the rest is history!

I completed my 28th year in public education in 2023. I spent five years in the classroom, a few years in transition positions, and then 16 years as a campus principal. You can probably tell by now that I didn't go back home and open a daycare. No, as that first year progressed, I started to learn more, get more comfortable, and notice my students starting to understand what I was teaching. That first year ended, and

I signed my contract for the next year and could not have been happier! As a classroom teacher, I was doing everything that I saw my past teachers doing while creating a learning environment that encouraged all students to engage with the learning, apply what they learned, and believe they could do big things in life. As an administrator, I continued with these strategies, realizing that I was now not only affecting a single classroom of students but a full school of little bodies, a group of motivated and growing teachers, and communities that jumped on board with my vision. Together we developed learning communities that ensured student growth and success. It was the hardest, greatest job I have ever loved!

28 years in this profession has taught me so much. So many different experiences developed my skills as not only a teacher but also as a leader who was valued and trusted in the communities in which I worked. I could share some stories that would shock you…and others that would melt your heart. I would not have changed a single one of them. Each of them made me approach life and my work differently as I became a life-long learner. I will say, however, that there are a few lessons that I learned along the way that I am compelled to share with you here. My goal is to encourage teachers worldwide to take the strategies and proven processes from this book and use them as they develop their own love of this profession. The world needs GREAT teachers! Our communities need GREAT teachers. And our students need people like you to believe in them and vow to do whatever you can to instill the belief that no matter what, they matter, and they can do whatever they set out to do in life!

You haven't taught until they have learned.

I remember my first years of teaching and the number of curriculum documents and teacher-edition textbooks that lined up my shelves. Then we must consider the fact that Texas was one of the first states to have accountability testing each year. So much to cover, so much for the students to learn, and so many ways they could be asked to apply their newly learned skills. If you stop to think about it, overwhelm definitely takes over! As professional educators, we all know we are required to teach all the curriculum each year, no matter how many skills are involved (I remember thinking how there were more skills to cover than days available to teach). I have seen so many teachers each year cover the skills, staying on course to complete the curriculum by specific deadlines mandated by states and districts. I have also seen times when the students had to perform on assessments based on what teachers had covered but the data proved that students didn't actually understand the skills quite the way the teacher had anticipated they would. As I had conversations with these teachers (and even myself over the years), I would hear, "But I taught it."

Teaching and learning are both an art. As teachers, we need to teach the way students learn, and that is where skill comes in. Yes, so many times we cover material, but I truly have learned that if the students did not learn it at a level that allows them to apply the learning to anything put in front of them, we didn't actually teach it. In my first few years, I had plans to cover so much learning, and I accomplished that task. But when my students didn't perform as I had planned on the state assessments, I had to reassess my teaching methods. I had to make changes in how I was delivering the materials. I had to realize that I was missing a piece of the puzzle that was hindering their progress, and it was all about student progress.

Curriculum is key…covering skills is important. To be that champion for your students, be sure you know exactly how your students are progressing, the ways in which they learn best, and use your data to determine if you taught them in a way that they truly learned. When you conquer this task, your teaching skills will soar, and you will see those lightbulbs go off in every one of your students' eyes!

Relationships are the most important part of your job!

If you have a student who is struggling at home and gets left behind often, how do you handle it? Are you one of those who mirror my first-grade teacher? I am not saying give up your own family/life obligations to take care of your students every day. I am saying that you can make stressful situations for kids so much better when they see you, their teacher whom they know and trust, check in on them and wait with them as the office staff locate their family, or just give them that little pat on the arm indicating that it will be ok.

Building a relationship with each of your students will ensure that every one of them will perform at their highest level. I remember having a conversation with someone during my time in the classroom. This person asked me how it was that I was able to work with some of the most challenged students (I was the grade-level ESL teacher working with children who spoke, read, and wrote mainly in Spanish) and get them to be successful on the curriculum each year. My response? It was the relationship! They knew I cared about them. They knew I wanted them to be successful. They knew that the classroom was a safe space to take academic risks. They knew that I would do everything I could to help them achieve what they dreamed of if they did their part as well. That was the relationship that I built with them. That was my overarching goal each year.

As an administrator, I spoke with a lot of students who were having difficulty in the classroom. Do you want to know what the most popular response was when I asked them why they were having trouble? Many students told me that they felt that their teacher did not like them. In no situation do I believe that we need to be "friends" with our students, but these responses would break my heart. If kids don't think you like them, will they learn from you? Trust you to help them be their best? And more importantly, will they want to be in your classroom? Most of these students were the ones each year who would do everything they could to get out of the classroom and spend time in the office (usually in trouble) because they didn't want to be in that classroom environment.

Take the time to get to know your students. Build the relationships that you would have wanted with your teacher as a child. Sure, there are challenging students in your room and maybe you do not like them all, but they don't need to know that! Challenge yourself to find ways to compliment even the most challenging students. Develop topics that you could discuss with any child, letting them feel that they are important enough to have conversations with you. And, most importantly, find a way to adopt the philosophy that every child is capable of learning…not necessarily in the same way on the same day…but all capable of progressing nonetheless!

Teachers need other teachers.

I remember that the most challenging part of my first year, when I knew nothing and was struggling just to make it through the day, was that I felt so isolated. I did not need someone to be in my room all day every day, holding my hand through every experience I encountered, but I did need someone to share their knowledge and expertise with me along my path so that I could learn how to incorporate their skills into my own teaching style.

Collaboration is key! So many of us tend to take our lesson plans, walk into our classrooms, shut the door, and do it all on our own, only seeking out help when we are at a point of truly struggling and wanting to quit altogether. What if we changed this? What if we made collaboration a normal part of teaching? What if we learn from and support each other early on before things go sideways? I believe in the power of collaboration. I know that without the teams that I was able to work with over the years, the ones who freely shared what worked each day and then learned how to adapt that to my own job responsibilities each year, I would have considered quitting more often than just during the first year in the classroom.

Find your tribe! Build your network! Learn from others! Ask questions! Share what you learn and discover what works with your students. This is what a true Professional Learning Community is. Embrace the support and use everything you learn to help you be your best. I know you deserve it…and your students do as well!

Teachers changed my life. I vowed to be one of those superheroes, and looking back on my career in education, I can confidently say I accomplished that. I left a legacy…one that put students first, one where I was able to pass on knowledge and wisdom to those in the profession, and one that allowed me to enjoy the hardest job you will ever love! Former students reach out to me often. Former students have approached me for their first teaching positions. Was I a champion for my students? Only my students can answer that, but I will say, the impact has been tremendous…not only for them but for me as well!

Margie Steinberg

https://www.linkedin.com/in/margie-steinberg-78643526/
https://www.facebook.com/margie.steinberg
https://www.instagram.com/steinberg2222/

My educational background is a BS from Wartburg College and MA from Drake University. Teaching experience ranges from Elementary Art to Reading and Language Arts in Tama and Mason City, Iowa. I've also been an instructor for North Iowa Area Community College, Drake University, Morningside College and Buena Vista University as well as Performance Learning Systems as the Iowa Coordinator. After 45 years of experience, I retired. My husband is Gene, children Chad and Stacy, and stepson Jim plus seven grandchildren. Member of Trinity Lutheran Church and Alpha Delta Kappa. Love to sing, craft and read.

TEACHING WITH HEART

By Margie Steinberg

Influences in one's life are extremely important. For me, a big part of who I am comes from the influence of my parents. In retrospect, they were the best teachers I had in my life. They taught me the importance of having a good work ethic and how to strive to be the best I could be. I remember my mom telling us we were brilliant, and we believed her! I was lucky to grow up in an environment that nurtured us. Farm life was a simpler way of life back then. Growing up in a small community that valued us was a cherished experience. Everyone knew us and helped along the way.

I actually thought I wanted to be a nurse like my two cousins. I ultimately found out that nursing was not for me. In high school, I had a teacher as a junior and senior that inspired me. I remember thinking I wanted to be an English teacher just like her someday. When I started college, my path was clear. Back then, we didn't have the practicums that students have today. My first experience with students was student teaching where I worked with high school and junior high ages. I knew then that I had made the right choice. Teaching was for me.

After college, I had an interview in Tama, Iowa for an elementary art position. Art was my minor, so I didn't think I had much of a chance. I remember sitting in the superintendent's office for the final leg of the interview. He said that usually someone with only a minor would not be considered, but he liked what my references said about me, and the job was mine. Needless to say, I was more prepared to teach English, but I took on the challenge. What a unique experience for this small-town girl with limited diversity in my very Norwegian community. I worked with the Meskwaki Indians and a principal who had the best heart imaginable. For two years, I worked with supportive staff and wonderful students who I thoroughly enjoyed teaching. It allowed me to expand that part of my soul. Interestingly enough, years later my parents took a trip to Oregon to visit relatives and rode the Amtrak Rails. In the smoking car, my dad struck up a conversation with a man who was from Tama! As they talked, Dad mentioned that he had a daughter who taught in Tama. The man remarked that he remembered me because his grandchildren talked about the wonderful art teacher they had. His kind comments certainly fed my soul and my dad's as well.

After moving to Mason City, I worked as a substitute teacher for a year. I had been offered a job in a bank, but decided I needed to stay with my teaching plan. I took on many sub jobs and finally got a call from the Personnel Director telling me he was going to get me "that job." I would be teaching language arts, speech, and drama at Monroe Junior High. Having no experience with speech and drama, I went to the University of Northern Iowa, stayed with some friends, and took some courses to be certified. I often wondered what I was getting myself into at that point! I took the positions of two teachers who very kindly left me files to get started. I will never forget what they did for me at that time when I needed help the most. I stayed at that junior high for 10 years until they closed the building.

My next position was at Roosevelt Middle School in Mason City where I ended up with a family of colleagues like I had before. As I look back on my career, I realize I had so many nurturing influences in my life from principals who cared about us to colleagues who wanted to work for the good of the students. I learned a valuable lesson when we moved to one middle school and put Roosevelt and John Adams together. It was the most challenging year of my career. Not enough was done to bring faculty and students together, and there were too many discipline problems that arose. Teachers and students work as a community, and that certainly didn't happen in this instance. The next adventure came when the district put the eighth grade and seventh grade into separate buildings for two years. We were fortunate in our seventh-grade building to have a principal who valued each of us and the students as well. Relatively few problems arose, and the faculty worked together to create an atmosphere conducive to learning for all students.

Along the way, I got my Master's Degree from Drake University in Effective Teaching. Getting a master's opened many doors for me. I was privileged to teach courses for Buena Vista University in the education program where I could take my experience in the classroom and give back to individuals that wanted to get into the teaching profession. Nominations by students earned me the Faculty of the Year award several times. I also taught for Performance Learning Systems which offered unique courses through Drake for teachers. For 11 years, I was the Iowa Coordinator for the program. I was privileged to work with instructors around the state who were extremely dedicated to the profession and desired to bring excellent experiences to teachers in our profession. I hope that countless individuals benefited from my experience in the teaching world through all these opportunities.

After retirement, I worked at North Iowa Community College for four years. I started a reading program there and worked one-on-one with students in the Mastery Writing Lab. I was fortunate to work with many foreign students who needed help in English. I was lucky to forge many unique friendships with the students and I earned the Excellence in Teaching Award while working there because a student nominated me…it was the highest praise for me as an instructor.

Was it the right decision to stay with teaching? I would have to say an overwhelming YES to that question. For 45 years, I was an educator in a profession I loved. One of the hardest decisions I had to make was retirement. In this day and age when educators question how effective they are in the classroom, I would have to say I taught at the optimum time to experience the euphoria that comes with success in the classroom. I love the fact that former students have become friends now. I even kept all those notes my students wrote me over the years. I value the importance of students in my life - they have impacted me in more ways than I ever dreamed possible. The truth is that one doesn't necessarily get wealthy by teaching, but the wealth comes in different ways. I wouldn't trade my experiences for anything else. Teaching became a way of life, and I hope that my life as a teacher is exemplified through the quote from Carl W. Buechner: "They may forget what you said, but they will never forget how you made them feel." I hope that my students felt valued in the classroom with me as their teacher.

Lessons learned from teaching...

Be flexible. Lessons will not always go as planned. We need to learn from our mistakes. I do remember several times that I had planned a lesson and in my head knew how it was to be executed. However, halfway through the lesson, I stopped and simply said, "This is just not working!" At this point, one needs to stop on a dime and use that flexibility and creativity to direct in a different way.

Share great ideas with others. I was told by a principal in my second year of teaching that I needed to talk to another teacher because I was going to be teaching seventh-grade language arts. Like a good new teacher, I talked to the seasoned teacher. Her response to me was that she worked for her material, and I could work for mine. I was speechless. Needless to say, I worked and worked to make the experience for my students the best it could be. I never forgot that lesson. When a new teacher came to me for help, I opened my files and invited them in. I never wanted anyone else to experience that kind of rejection.

Be able to admit you are wrong. We'd like to think that everything that comes out of our mouths is the right answer. Sometimes that's not true! The students will respect you more because you can admit that you don't know it all.

Students need to experience. Lectures may set up a lesson, but as a teacher, there comes a time when you need to step back and let your students take the reins. They will be better learners because of this. Students need to be active, self-directed learners. Modeling what you want out of an assignment is good for you as a teacher and the students' understanding as well. I've had several poems published, and when we studied that genre in language arts, I read the poems to the class. I love to sing and there were even times when I got to do that for the students as well! When students needed to do a speech, I modeled how I would do it first. Did I want them all to be just like me? No! Doing a speech can be really intimidating for a student, so I wanted to show them how I would organize and present. When we put ourselves "out there," the students will feel more likely to do the same.

Laugh! Laughter brings joy. The classroom needs to be a place that is safe for students, and laughter helps. There are probably times that students laughed at me because of something that I said or did, but I hope they laughed with me more.

Let students know you love teaching. Your passion should come through in every lesson. For some, it's a job; for most, I hope it's a profession to be nurtured and cared for as you work with students. I remember a student stopping before leaving the classroom and saying to me, "You really like what you do, huh?"

A positive climate in the classroom is so important. Shouting at students gets a teacher nowhere. We can admit that we've done our fair share of that when frustrated. Think before you do, and it will be easier to deal with students in a positive manner.

Show students you are human. I remember when my dad died I was so distraught. Students empathized with me and showed me so much compassion as I struggled with this in my own life. We don't always have a good day, and admitting that can help everyone cope. Students will feel freer to share when they are experiencing pain in return. Being compassionate and empathetic with students is paramount to maintaining a good climate in the classroom.

Establish relationships with students. It's important to get to know students before delving into the content. Your perception of the students is so important to know how to approach them as you prepare lessons to be learned. It would be wonderful to think that a teacher would like every student in the classroom. Unfortunately, that is not always the case. There will be those students who simply rub you the wrong way. In a class I taught for Performance Learning Systems, the 2 X 10 method really struck a chord with me. Find the student that gets under your skin and for 10 days, take two minutes to engage them in conversation. When I did this, I found a new common ground with the student, and many times this individual became a favorite. We need to find ways to form relationships in the classroom so learning can be optimized.

Give respect to get respect. We hear so often today that students don't show respect to others or teachers. Teachers model how this is to happen by showing respect to all. It's really incredible how much we model in the classroom…sometimes good and sometimes bad. Again, it's important to think before saying or doing.

> *"A teacher affects eternity; he/she can never tell where his/her influence stops"* —Henry Brooks Adams.

After all these years, there are former students that I see that remind me of something that I said or did or they did in the classroom. I love that these are not forgotten. A student shared with me that I told him to use his "loud voice for influence instead of anger," and he remembers our little talk to this day. He also said that I told him that "if you don't believe in yourself, no one else will." These are the moments that students remember, and I treasure that my influence might have made a difference. Years ago, a former student stopped me in a store and asked if she could show me something. Out of her billfold, she took a piece of paper that had been opened and folded many times because it showed the wear. The note said that I believed in her and knew she would do great things someday. I remembered how quiet she was in my classroom. She had kept that note after all those years. I looked at her, hugged her, and told her how much that meant to me! Wow! We don't know how even the smallest snippet of kindness can affect students in our classroom even years later. I think of her more often now and how I was so glad that I wrote that note at the time. The rewards we get as teachers may be few after putting in so many years, but instances like this make me swell with pride that I chose a profession that I love.

We are life-long learners. I love the fact that I can learn something new after all these years. I hope that my lessons in the classroom were innovative and creative. Thinking about what I wanted students to know and be able to do was at the forefront of how I planned. Students may not think about nouns, verbs, spelling, or reading comprehension, but these concepts shape how they work with their thinking in some way.

For me, teaching was a way of life. I had my kids at home and my kids at school. I miss the interactions with colleagues and students. I miss the unpredictability that often comes when dealing with students. I miss all the activities that were generated with a faculty that cared about students. I miss having great administrators who cared for faculty and students. I miss the laughter and loudness in the hallways. I miss the high fives that students so freely gave. I miss the anticipation of starting a new school year and closing down the building for the next. These are the wonderful memories that I have after teaching for 45 years. Lucky me!

Dr. Rachel Alex

CEO and Founder of HELP in Schools LLC

https://www.linkedin.com/in/drrachelalex/
https://www.facebook.com/profile.php?id=61557630260811
https://www.instagram.com/helpinschools
https://helpinschools.org/

As a strategic leader with a proven track record in educational leadership, I've dedicated over twenty years to fostering positive school cultures and uplifting community spirit.

My school district roles have ranged from Instructional Coach to Executive Director, each strengthening my expertise in project leadership, performance evaluation, and systems management. Upholding values of accountability and collaboration, I am committed to advancing district excellence and community well-being.

My educational foundation is extensive, with a Doctorate in Educational Leadership complemented by ongoing professional development through esteemed educational associations. This academic pursuit is matched by my practical efforts to build morale and drive forward-thinking initiatives that prioritize student success.

My ability to forge meaningful connections has always been pivotal in cultivating a supportive and progressive learning environment. I actively embrace challenges, seeking out opportunities that prompt both personal and professional growth, with a steadfast focus on future-readiness and student achievement.

TEACHING IS LEARNING

By Dr. Rachel Alex

Funny, I never thought I would become an educator. After moving to a small town with limited job opportunities that would lead to a promising career, I signed up to be a substitute teacher. That one-time experience inspired me to become a math teacher. Twenty-five years later, I am still an educator, only my students are campus and district leaders.

I began my career in education in 1999. I was hired during the middle of the school year while on maternity leave. I was so excited about the opportunity and could not wait to begin my new career as an educator.

I look back and laugh at how I entered my classroom with a few posters that I joyfully bought from the teacher supply store, several pens, highlighters, and no clue of what I was getting myself into. As I was given the day to set up my classroom and prepare for my new class, I was informed that my students were challenging, and they had already scared off three substitutes. Neighboring teachers stopped by to introduce themselves and let me know that if I needed anything, they would be right there to help.

I loved math, so I thought that teaching math would come naturally.

My teaching assignment was 7th grade math and math intervention. The students who were in math intervention were not successful on the state exam the year before and therefore were assigned a second math class. Fortunately, that meant I only had to teach two different lessons each day.

As I reviewed my colorful teacher edition of the textbook, I recall filling in my teacher lesson plan book with lesson objectives, page numbers, which problems to solve, and homework assignments. By the end of the day, I was several weeks ahead of what both the students and I were going to do.

I was so nervous when the bell rang and students began to enter my classroom. The students walked in with confidence and certainty of what to expect. I began by introducing myself and getting to know them. Time passed quickly between classes; I was exhausted but ready to start the next day teaching.

The second day with students was somewhat different than the first. A variety of students approached me with comments like "I hope you stay," "I'm glad you came back," and "Let's see how long you last."

The bell rang and I was ready! My mindset was, "It's showtime!"

I asked the students to open their books and turn to the assigned page on the board. Students looked at me and stared. Finally, a student said, "What book?"

I said, "Your textbook." They again stared at me, and the brave student said, "We don't have a book." I was now embarrassed and unprepared for what to do next. So, I began to ask questions of the students. After a disturbing discussion, I realized that I now had to wing it because all of the lesson plans were null and void.

At the end of that long day, I went home tired but also so disappointed in myself. I repeatedly asked myself, *why didn't I know? What do I do now?*

I was ashamed to ask other teachers what to do. I was telling myself that they would think I was an idiot and didn't deserve to be a teacher. I was wrong. I was first given apologies followed by lots of support. By the end of that first week, I knew what resources I had access to, the ones I needed, and how to get them. *I'm ready*, or so I thought.

I was prepared and I knew my content. I taught tirelessly from bell to bell every day. At the end of the week, I was ready to give my students their first quiz. The results were awful. My heart was broken. Most of my students failed. I didn't understand what happened. I taught and taught the content. I showed them how to solve and write equations. What happened? So, I taught it again. I taught harder, from bell to bell. I assigned more homework for practice so they would be ready to retake the quiz. After an intensive reteach, again the majority of the students failed. I was unsuccessful and so were my students.

Soon after the results came out, the students began doing what they were good at - disruption!

I disappointed them and myself. I was teaching, but they weren't learning.

I started asking myself reflective questions like:

What did I expect them to do?
What questions did they ask me?
What questions did I ask them?
Where did they get stuck?
Why didn't they show their work?
When did they practice?
What did they practice?
Did the quiz align with what they were doing in class?

Sadly, I did not have a response to any of my questions. This later served as a guide for lesson planning. My lesson planning took on a two-fold approach; what was I teaching and how would they learn it?

This process took a lot longer than I thought because I had to consider learning from the student's point of view. After doing this for several weeks, my learning and performance improved.

The more I engaged with the students, the more I learned about them. I naively assumed that students were prepared for the content. I taught whole group lessons to all students. I didn't know anything about differentiation. How was I supposed to know what they didn't know?

At this point, my frustration was high! I was burning out, exhausted. Some of my students were learning, but I was failing the others.

I finally asked for help.

I observed a high-performing teacher. She also had high-performing students. My students weren't at their performance level, but what I noticed was the many ways she facilitated learning. There were small groups, manipulatives, group work, peer tutoring, and lots of discussion among the students. Her class was structured, inviting, and fun. I wanted to be there. I wanted my students to feel this way about my class. I wanted my students to enjoy learning. I then realized that I did not plan for the engagement.

Now my lesson planning took on a three-pronged approach: teaching, learning, and engagement.

After a few more observations and co-planning with my new mentor, my class was moving in the right direction. Expectations were starting at the threshold of the classroom. I talked less, they talked more. I asked questions, they answered questions. I had frequent checks for understanding, and they began to recognize when they became confused. I provided examples, they delivered evidence of mastery. I had created a learning environment.

It was not perfect, but it was far better than before.

The majority of the students were excelling at a rapid rate. They were making connections to prior learning and were able to demonstrate and explain their thinking. But there were still some students that I was struggling to reach. They required more support. Oftentimes, their behavior would get in the way, and they would end up not completing any work. I thought they didn't care, and I wasn't going to let them ruin the class for everyone else. So, I decided to ignore them and leave them alone.

One day my mentor teacher asked me how certain students were doing in my class. I explained that they didn't care, so I left them alone. She began giving me some background on these students and I was crushed.

How was I supposed to know?

The next day, I stopped leaving them alone and started building a relationship. It was small things like acknowledging them, thanking them, giving them ways to successfully and safely participate, and any other thing I could think of to make them feel part of the class. I was seeing positive changes in their behavior. Even on bad days, it wasn't as bad anymore.

I remember one day we were learning about angles. This one opportunity (challenging student) appeared to like this topic. He wasn't putting anything on paper, but he was able to answer questions and explain his thinking every time he volunteered and when called upon. My heart was beaming! The students were asking him questions, and he was so proud to explain why it was so easy.

I was so excited about his participation and learning that I decided to make a positive call home. I introduced myself and explained to the dad that I was his son's math teacher. He angrily asked me, "What the 'f' did he do now?" I went on to brag about his son's progress in math, highlighting his outstanding understanding of angles and how his thinking helped so many of the other students in the class. I poured it on thick! The father said, "Alright, thank you."

I wasn't sure how to feel after we hung up. I believed I did the right thing and would do it again. I just wanted to celebrate him. He deserved it!

The next day, the student came up to me and said, "I heard you called my house." I nodded. He said, "Thank you," and smiled.

It was worth it! He was worth it!

Over the years, I have had many experiences with my students. I've rejoiced, cried, and laughed. Some days were better than others, but every day mattered.

That first year of teaching was hard because I didn't realize that it was my first year of learning too. I arrogantly thought that because I was good at math I would be good at teaching it. Knowing the content is only half the battle. Knowing my students made me a better teacher. I learned to recognize where they were with readiness for content and how to scaffold learning and make it meaningful. I learned to change my perspective on teaching by first understanding what the learning should look like. I learned to ask for help. I learned that student learning measures teaching efficacy.

I became an educator because of limited geographic opportunities. I remained an educator because it mattered. It still matters. Besides being a mother, it is one of the most meaningful things I do.

Joanne de la Garza

Joanne de la Garza is a dedicated educator who sees herself daily in the children she serves. The Houston native still resides in the barrio she grew up in and loves. She spends her time reading, drawing, and watching fútbol with her husband and three kids.

THIS IS MY WHY

By Joanne de la Garza

"Hi, my name is Joanne and I'm a teacher." The moment I meet someone new and I make this introduction their immediate question is, "Why?" My response of "I don't know," tends to cause a stir, but it's the truth. Growing up I NEVER planned on becoming a teacher. I never made my friends or cousins play school, and I definitely did not envy my teachers and their cheesy jokes. To be 100% honest, I wanted to do forensic psychology and become an FBI agent. Crazy right? I wish I had an amazing "How I Became a Teacher" story for you with all the beautiful images of rainbows, fairies, and unicorns….ok maybe that's a bit much, but you get the picture. That, however, is not my story. In reality, I legit fell into teaching.

One day, out of the blue, my former high school assistant principal reached out to a mutual friend. He needed college students to serve as math tutors for his middle school, and lucky me got asked. After a five-minute phone conversation a few days later I showed up to work, barely nineteen years old wearing tattered jeans, a band concert t-shirt, and my trusty Chuck Taylors having never worked a day in my life. I was in for quite the ride. Nearly two decades later, you'll still find me in a math classroom rocking my trusty Chuck Taylors. Something about that environment hooked me - and good.

Now, I'd love to tell you everything was a breeze, but we all know teaching is hard. When you're teaching you are always "on." Everything you do within that school building is being watched and listened to. In those four walls that have your name on the door, students expect you to know everything. You are their source of truth and the standard by which they will lead themselves throughout the day. You have all this power to mold and influence these kids. A lot is riding on you. I tell my husband all the time that I'm so mentally tired.

Why? Teaching is making a million decisions a day and anticipating what will happen as a result of those decisions. It's being responsible for 40+ little brains and hearts. There are some days I dread going to work. I contemplate reasons to stay home and I count down the days until the next break. It sounds horrible, I know. But it's true. Teaching takes hard work and isn't for the faint. Kids can be mean. Parents can be mean. Administration can be mean. The list of things to do is a mile long. Teaching takes thick skin and perseverance.

New teachers ask after all these years why I still do it. Now, it's taken me a while to finally put this into words, but to be completely transparent, it goes back to how I got started. Teaching, like child-rearing, takes a village. And my village was made up of Libby, Misty, and Lynne. There were SO many more but these three ladies personified three great ideals that have stayed with me this whole time, and I'd like to share them with you.

Life is short; Math is fun.
Teaching shouldn't be stressful; chillax.
Never lower your standards for anyone.

For Libby, life was short and math was fun. That's how she lived, and that's how I'll always remember her. She was a young, new teacher who loved math, was outgoing, and was passionate about kids learning. She thought outside the box and unconventionally went about instruction. We took class outside and did hands-on activities that onlookers would have thought looked like playing. No, we were learning. She knew her curriculum inside out, and she had a knack for knowing what misconceptions her students would have. Then she made fun games and silly, rhyming mnemonic devices to help foster learning. She was always stepping on toes and I feared she would push too far but she would remind me that "Math is fun." To this day, I find myself incorporating parts of the lessons she taught in her 6th-grade class with my own classes. I remember them and smile and say a little "Thank you," and push forward with my lesson. Libby, you are so missed.

If Libby was the new, outgoing, always moving teacher, Misty was, for me at least, quite the opposite. She was calm, cool, and level-headed. She was an established teacher who had been teaching the upper grades for quite some time. She was known for being strict but fair and for knowing her math. I remember meeting her for the first time and was blown away by how smart and funny she was. She showed me that math could be hard but could also be broken down into chunks and tackled piece by piece. I would stress out about everything we needed to cover and everything my students still didn't know how to do, and she would tell me, "Chillax." She helped me notice when it was time to focus on my mental health, take breaks, and make sure I remembered to tell myself that teaching shouldn't be stressful. On those days I contemplate getting out of bed, I take a few deep breaths and repeat that mantra - chillax.

Thanks to these two wonderful ladies, I was able to plan effective and engaging lessons and prioritize my mental health so that I could continue to stand before my classroom and lead. They fueled me as a teacher, but Lynne fueled me as a person. She loved on me and never let me bring myself down. She helped me find my motivation so that I could continue to push myself and my students. She showed me that everyone should be held accountable regardless of their situation. She showed me that you should never lower your standards for anyone. Students will rise to the standards you place for them. We should be there to guide them. She pushed her students hard but never once let them use excuses to get out of anything. She made kids learn to be organized, ask for help when they needed it, and take ownership of their future. I heard many students tell her she was strict, upon other not-so-nice words, but they loved her for pushing them. She was relentless but her students continuously rose to the occasion. She never let them down and she never let them quit. She molded them and she molded me, and I will forever be grateful for her.

So back to the question, "After all these years why do you still do it?" Easy; I do it so that one day I can be that Libby, Misty, or Lynne for someone else. I want to pay it forward. I do it for all the random hugs students give you when they sense you're feeling down. I do it for that smile when you tell them "Good morning." I do it for all the cute, misspelled letters that say "You're the best." I do it for the relationships you get to create and foster so your students feel so safe they accidentally call you "Mom," "Momma," "Ma," or "Mami" when they need help. I can't even count the number of times my students have made me cry with their acts of love, empathy, and sense of caring. I do it for the times I realize that I messed up and need to be the bigger person and apologize to a nine-year-old. It's OK because I'm teaching them that they have feelings and deserve respect as well. I do it for all the small victories my students get to celebrate. I do it for the "Aha!" moments. Seeing my students' faces light up when it finally all makes sense. When they realize all their hard work was worth it.

After almost two decades in education, I can finally say that teaching for me was a calling. It molded me and shaped my life. I tell those who'll listen that I don't know anything else. Teaching has been and will be my life. Every year I start over with a new group of kids who I get the privilege of loving and growing with. It sounds cheesy but it's my truth. I bust my butt daily making sure my kids feel loved. Every student who walks through my classroom door will know that Mrs. De La Garza loves them. I tell them daily. I show them daily. I hold myself to that truth and standard. I may not like some of the things they do, say, or how they treat me or others, but I won't stop loving them. I greet them good morning and I wish them good luck. They are my loves and my love-sicles. Mis amores.

Jennifer Weeks

www.facebook.com/jennifer.flemingweeks?mibextid=ZbWKwL
https://twitter.com/HheWeeks51089

During her childhood, Jennifer Weeks moved frequently with her family due to her father's job in engineering. She's lived in Phoenix, Venezuela, Aruba, and Houston. Living in different places has shown her that all people of diverse backgrounds strive to make connections with others. In her spare time, she wrote short stories and created plays with her younger siblings.

Jennifer became a teacher as a second career. She went back to school in her later 30s, and graduated with a teaching degree from University of Houston Downtown. She worked at a Title 1 school in Sheldon for 6 years. During that time, she worked at building relationships and making her students a top priority. She continues to do this, and strives for excellence among herself and students. When she is not educating young minds, her hobbies include: spending time with her family and dogs, road trips, and cooking.

PATHWAY TO PURPOSE

By Jennifer Weeks

There I was, watching my baby brother graduate from Texas Tech University. My one-year-old son is sitting in my lap; my ten-year-old daughter is silently reading a Percy Jackson book for the fourth time. What was I doing? I was stuck again. I was nearing 40 years old, working at a dentist's office. I wanted to be something important. My dreams of being a dental hygienist were lost when I tore a disc in my neck early in my dental assisting career. I was lost in the shuffle of motherhood and work. It was after that trip that I decided to go back to school, but what should I do? Fortunately for me, the college near the town I lived in offered a full, four-year bachelor program along with night classes. IF I wanted to become a teacher. Did I?

It was not my first choice. As a young 20-something-year-old at Texas State University (formerly Southwest Texas when I attended there), I took a career test. The top careers listed for me were: dental hygienist, psychologist, and teacher. Under each career, the annual salary was listed, and I thought that becoming a dental hygienist was the best choice for me because the salary was higher than the others. I attended some courses and partied a little (maybe a lot). I met the man of my dreams. I then moved home and got married. I was barely 23 years old. I told myself I would finish college after marriage. Then, I became a dental assistant (to see if I really wanted to be in the dental field). I loved it! It was fast-paced, demanding, and I helped people. I especially loved the pediatric patients! I had a way of calming the most anxious kids. But then, it happened. I tore a disc in my neck. Besides the excruciating pain that was searing down my neck and into my left arm, I cried even more for my dreams of becoming a dental hygienist. My doctor told me my neck would never properly heal. I would need surgery; I didn't want to spend my life in pain. Due to the pain of the torn disc, I started working in the front office and handling insurance and billing. That is when I became stuck. I was unchallenged and lost my purpose for 12 years. Then, I watched my brother graduate.

Going back to school at 38 was insane. Nursing a baby, taking care of two kids, and working full time at a dentist's office proved to be pretty challenging. I had so many credits to transfer and classes to retake. Chemistry, geology, and sacrificing every eight hours on Saturday for a biology class with a lab. Finally, I received my associate's degree! My basics were finished, and it was time to get into the teaching courses. I entered my first track of teaching, and I was a nervous wreck. I took classes part time at night while continuing to work at the dentist's office during the day. Yet, I still made it to my daughter's soccer games on the weekend. When we traveled to Disney World in the summer, I submitted work online.

Finally, during the last semester, the full time student teaching was about to start. My colleagues and my friends that I took two years of classes with were huddled together outside every week, talking about our future careers and our struggles balancing school and home life. Some were single parents working two jobs trying to make ends meet, some were young and single, and some, like me, were going back to school as a second career path. Most of them were placed at the same school to do their student teaching. I was placed at a different school. To say I was nervous would be an understatement. I was about to be a student teacher for a second-grade class.

That semester was one of the busiest and most demanding three months of my life. Teaching, lesson planning, parenting, and exams. Yikes, it was challenging. Graduation was looming around the corner. I could hardly wait to hold that degree in my hand and wear that cap and gown. Many of my cohorts already had promises of working at the same campus where they had been a student teacher. That's what I wanted too. I would've loved something familiar where I already knew the students and the faculty. That did not happen. So, I created a teaching portfolio and a professional resume. I drove to schools and personally handed out my resume. I introduced myself, and I had interviews. It finally happened. The day I lost my voice before one of these interviews was the day I got my first teaching job. Finally, I got a job as a 4th-grade reading teacher! But was I good enough? Would my students like me? Would my students learn? These are the questions that anxiously hovered around me like a thick fog. I already knew it would be stressful. I knew that the demands of teaching were tough. Friends and colleagues alike shared tales of the challenges they faced. One of my friends, Kara, would be grading papers during soccer practice almost every night. However, I did feel slightly prepared. I had half a year of student teaching and observations and substitute taught in the spring. I told myself, regardless of everything else, that I would make my first year in the classroom as a rookie teacher fun.

To say I surprised myself that year was an understatement. After the initial awkwardness of getting into the groove of teaching, the growing pains dissipated. I was able to find a system that worked for me. Believe it or not, the goal I gave myself actually worked! I did find enjoyment in the craziness of my first year, but it was so much more than that. While I was learning and growing, I worked with my 4th-grade team, and we created numerous projects and storytelling foldables. We read books aloud and then created lessons centered around the story. We used markers and construction paper, played games that involved movement around the classroom, and did fun activities like "plot dances." My confidence started building as well as my students'. I saw them grow academically. However, through all of the trials and tribulations of my first year, the one thing that stands out the most is the relationships I built with my students. What caught me by surprise was how much I would love and care for each of my students. Our classroom became our family.

"I love you Mrs. Weeks. I will miss you so much. You are the best teacher. You are the best teacher I ever had. You were always there for me when I needed you, even when I was disrespectful to you. You were always nice to me……". Tears pour down my face every time I read this letter. This was from my 5th-grade student last year. Her name is *Josie.

Josie came to my class mid-year after leaving other schools in the district (for various reasons). She told stories about her mom who told her about sex at a young age. Her dad, whom she witnessed in the act of intercourse. Her grandpa cursed at her and called her worthless. She was inappropriately sexual with classmates. She passed notes with explicit drawings, cussed and yelled, and had some learning disabilities. She saw the counselor regularly. Regardless of her upbringing, she was a beautiful soul. She longed to feel special like any child deserves to be nurtured and cared for. She asked for these things by acting out, yelling, and being inappropriate with classmates. I worked with her, gave her some patience, and even when she would say, "I'm bad," I would tell her she just needed to make better choices. She formed an attachment to me. I watched her gain trust in me. Once trust and a relationship were built, she started working harder in class.

She started the year by saying she couldn't read (she was dyslexic). By March, her growth was remarkable. She would read full chapter books, write in a journal, and check her work. She still didn't work well with partners, and she preferred to work at the teacher's table. I let her. She loved expressing her thoughts through writing and would frequently share her journal entries with me. I just wanted her to shine. And shine, she did.

5th grade is a year of transition, and in a Title 1 school, you sometimes see students who don't want to leave the comfort of their elementary classrooms and go to middle school. This was Josie. She spent the last day of the year in my homeroom. She didn't want to be in hers because the girls isolated her, and she didn't want the dirty looks and drama. That last day I received the letter…I remember that day as clear as a bell. It all started at dismissal. Students were packing up. Josie starts crying, begging, "Please don't let me go, Mrs. Weeks." Our hall monitors were loud and at her heels.

" Let's go!" She grabbed my arms and cried into my shirt. "You have to leave!" they said. My heart felt like it was being pulled in different directions. My teacher-mom instincts persevered.

I said, "I'm just going to walk with her down the hall, she's having a tough time." The counselor somehow knew she was there. She met her halfway down the hallway. That was the last time I saw her. Her letter stays on my fridge so I never forget how someone who seems like a lost cause can be positively influenced by the right mentor.

Josie's story is all about how building good relationships with students transforms your classroom environment and leads to positive behavior. Building relationships is crucial for more than one reason. First, it builds trust. It shows that I will be there for my students and their families whenever they have a concern or question. It also helps me, as a teacher, understand what is going on in their lives outside the classroom. It all starts with the first time I meet my student and their family. I try to find out what motivates them, and through the process of getting to know them, I start to build a relationship.

For example, every week I hold a "mystery student" lunch. During the week, I draw a name from my class list to be my mystery student. I tell my class that I have picked a mystery student, and I will not let them know who it is until the end of the day. As long as that student does not have any conduct marks, they can have lunch in my classroom. Sometimes I let them pick a friend. "Mystery student" benefits behavior and relationships. When students are sharing a meal in your class, you learn about their friends, families, hobbies, pets, and anything else they think is important to them. It's not a regular classroom setting with 20 or more students working, and my attention is on many different things. It's a small group sharing a relaxed lunch and talking.

Josie's story is just one of the many teacher/student relationships that I have formed over the years. One of the most rewarding experiences is when you see a student you have taught being successful and they tell you, "Thank you for teaching me and building my confidence," or "Because of you, I am in theater," or "I now love to read because you made me love books". This is just an example of some of the things I have been told during my career.

Teaching may not have been my first choice, but had I chosen a different path, I would have never experienced the joy of impacting so many young lives. This second chance gave my life a bigger purpose, and I can't wait to see where this journey will continue to lead.

S. Ursula Doyle

Founder & CEO of Angels Army Mobile Health and Wellness

https://www.linkedin.com/in/s-ursula-doyle-mba-sphr-18502225/
https://www.instagram.com/duffdoylellc/
https://angelsarmymhw.com

S. Ursula Doyle, is founder and single minority owner of Angels Army, a mobile health and wellness buisness. She is orginally from West Virginia but now Texas "branded" and a self proclaimed autodidact, lover of learning, mother of 3, HR professional turned Educator. Her current favorite pastime is riding her motorcycle named Royalty.

MY WHY: FINDING MY SEED

By S. Ursula Doyle

Well, to truly understand my "why," I've got to give a little background about me. I call myself a post-pandemic educator, as I am one of the thousands of people who migrated or were forced out of their occupations and given the *"opportunity"* (if you will) to try something new. I chose teaching as my pivot from 20+ years in human resources in the corporate world because it was something one of my colleagues said we should do together. To connect the dots, I had a family member (my great Aunt) who was a teacher all of her career. And it was her interactions with me when I was a kid from ages nine through 13 that made me have a disdain for teaching when I finally reached the age to decide what I wanted to do for a living.

To be REAL honest, I would tell teachers all the time that I admired them and the work that they did every day, but I knew I could not do what they did simply based on my own three kids that I sent to school and the challenges that I knew they must be facing teaching them. Then multiply that by all those other kids… whew!!! I knew it had to be a WORK from the heart, and I felt I did not possess those kinds of qualities. I was just not qualified!

So why now? What changed? How was a simple suggestion from my colleague enough for me to push past what I thought I knew about the teaching world and take the plunge (and I do mean plunge)?! Well, besides being burnt out with my current profession and the look back at my life to determine if I had made any real impact or changes in others' lives, I was getting to a certain age that made me scrutinize what was important and why I felt unfulfilled internally. At the end of my career in human resources, I started substituting at the school district near my house. I wanted to evaluate the waters to see if I could do it.

My schedule allowed me to sub on Fridays, so I began in 2019 by going to each school in that district. I took various opportunities from every campus and each level and subject area. I wanted to see where I would fit in and which group of students I would mesh with and have the most impact on. I made a few quick determinations during this process about what I did not want and could not tolerate which helped me when I did get to the point of saying, "Let me do this," but then COVID happened, and I was out until the end of the school year of 2020 (during which a lot had changed).

So, this girl, from the mountains of West Virginia who had so many interests growing up, could not figure out what she was good at or what was her talent despite having a real love for the sciences. The sciences have always intrigued me; it is the wonderings that get me, the mystery, and the exploration of it all. I say that because I look back at my life and I see the connections to how a tree grows from that seed that is placed in the ground. And here is the even crazier thing - as much as I love all the sciences, I ended up teaching ELA!!! What in the world? But there is a connection in all that we do, and I want to use this analogy of the process of growth in a tree to share how I feel it correlates with my life. These choices, whether looked upon as happen-stance or fate or just pure coincidence, do not have an influence on me because I chose to believe they were divine providence. Truly, the sciences prove it for me. Walk with me so I can show you how all these intricacies align to make up my seed (potential).

My Journey – The Planted Seed

Now, I would like to chat about my very intense journey to becoming a teacher. As I mentioned in my "why," I really had a two-fold reason for making this journey; however, when I made up my mind to do it, I had completed an upward and downward cycle of substituting at every campus in the district that I wanted to teach in. I knew by the time I started my ACP (Alternative Certification Program) that I wanted to teach at the elementary level, and I had basically set my mind that 1st grade would be my sweet spot. It was a thorough investigation of what campus culture I felt really good about and what level of students' behaviors and expectations I could "deal" with and not feel super overwhelmed. I can tell you honestly, I did not know what I was signing up for!

I am telling this part of my story for those who are thinking about becoming a teacher and did not take the traditional route by degree. These are things I wish I had known, or at least had someone share with me, so I could have had an RJP (Realistic Job Preview) into not only the journey but how the process does not end with just completing your ACP.

Okay, so choosing the ACP was a no-brainer for me (at the time, I only knew of one choice). I went through Region 4 and found it was very intentional and detailed. I started in February 2020, and the classes were fast-paced and back-to-back with no break. I was done with my online classes by late May but I was under the pressure of time to study and be approved to take the exam so I could be approved to teach by the school year that began in early August. I literally had no time to think about anything else but the goal! For me, it was a good thing but also a very intense process. I did it. I was able to complete all the study materials in 240 Tutoring (this is an application designed to give you a good determiner of whether you are sufficiently prepared to take the exam or not). It was hectic as you must finish, submit your proof of passing the practice tests, and then get registered to take the exam all with enough time to put into place to receive your results back in time to either start a job as a teacher or to retake the exam if you didn't pass any part of the exam. To top it off, I started this process the year Texas added the STR (Science of Teaching Reading) exam as a part of the minimal requirement of being a teacher, therefore, not only did I have to take my core exam (four hours of six content areas), but I also had to take a separate exam called the Science of Teaching Reading – STR (five hours). All before I could start the next phase of finding a job opportunity and start working to complete my hours toward being fully certified. Can I get a "Whew!!!" When I say I did not know if I was coming or going, standing up or sitting down - all of that was only the beginning of the "hard" part!!!

I want to stop right here and give a little bit of advice… this choice of joining the very elite membership of being an educator is not something that should be done with just a thought of good work hours and holidays and summers off because I will tell you right now, all this time you think you will have to just put your feet up and relax is a myth (particularly in your first two to three years). It is a commitment like no other that you will embark upon. You must know that your heart, time, and resources will be sucked into accomplishing this profession (that is, if you do it right). However, on the flip side, the payout is the most rewarding, life-altering, impactful thing that you will experience akin to being a parent. You are in for all kinds of excitement (up and down the chain of emotions).

All of the things I just mentioned were me planting my seeds in the soil of education. When you plant a seed, the amazing thing is that the seed goes into the ground and is covered up. The environment it is in causes this tiny thing to shed its coat, and then the roots come out and grow down first. In the life of the seed, as it is buried from the perspective above ground, it appears as if nothing is happening, leaving you wondering if what you put in the soil is going to produce anything. For weeks, in fact, it could be months, before anything can be seen above the ground. Oh, but underneath, there is much happening, lots of work! That is what I felt during all my coursework, the tests, and the waiting for the results of all my input to produce something. So, I say to you, do not get discouraged because seeds are going to do what they need to do; keep planting and stay hopeful!

I finished everything that was required of me, passing all the exams. Then one more thing was thrown at me - it was something called edTPA. The technical definition of it as per www.txnesinc.com is: "A performance-based, subject-specific assessment and support system used by educator preparation programs throughout the United States to emphasize, measure, and support the skills and knowledge that all teachers need from day one in the classroom." The short of it is a portfolio that I had submitted as an alternative or substitute for the PPR exam. All of which was more money, time, and targeted intentionality of documentation. I really thought I would lose my mind as I was going through all of this during my first year of teaching in addition to what you must do for the ACP during your internship. And that's not all. The district required certain coursework for all educators, and then finally the campus required items. I was soooo ill-prepared mentally for all it took to get to being a teacher to what it takes once you are a teacher. And guess what? I have not even mentioned the meat and potatoes of the job (the students and the curriculum). How about a double whew here (whew! whew!). In the words of my children and students when we are working on something that takes a lot of time and energy... *Are we done yet?!?!* The answer? No way!

I felt win after win, but guess what? In order to get win after win, I had to have test after test. There was challenge upon challenge, much like when the seed finally pushes its way through the soil. Can you believe it, a very tender binding of leaves and stem, pushing through this dense dirt to reach upward and outward? That amazes me! You will feel like you are failing or don't quite understand the lingo, what all is required of you, and wonder how you will ever keep up or manage it all on top of grasping the curriculum. There's figuring out how to really know if students are learning, what to do if they aren't learning, or what to do to reach all the various levels you will have within your room. This is the adjustment to the external elements. You're growing!

Realistic Job Preview (RJP)- The Sapling

All that leads me to my next topic…what it really looked like for me to be a teacher. I am currently in my third year, and I will tell you that I had been a part of a conversation with some other long-term teachers at one of the middle schools in our district while I was subbing. It stood out to me then as I could not really understand how the words that were shared with me were part of working in a public school. But boy do I know what they mean now. So, this is the tidbit of that conversation: "Working in education is so political; there is so much red tape." I will be really honest with you, as a mother of three grown children, I never saw the school system from that lens, and being on this side of it now, I see so much of why conversations such as that one were being had by folks within this profession. I will say that if your leadership is transparent, you can be sure you will encounter it with no filter or protection. However, I have been under a couple of different leadership positions within my campus as well as in the district, and prior to the change, I felt sheltered from that whole political mindset of the reasons for decisions within the job. I always knew that change in leadership changes culture and the outcome of how things are done, but I was not prepared for the surmounting issues that come from the "politics" of the job being front and center.

To do this job, you must keep in mind that *change* is a permanent part of the job description. Being flexible, resourceful, and capable of dealing with challenges and adjusting/pivoting whenever necessary. The students are and should be the centerpiece of what we do every day; however, many moving parts will pull you in various directions, especially in the first couple of years. I do not know if I will ever become acclimated to how much time it requires to be a teacher, but I will say that I know it is extremely hard to turn off the switch once it is on. I have come home night after night, and this is what I dream about when I lay my head down. My conversations have been about my students, what is going on in the profession, what I need to do, how our grade level can grow as a team, how my lessons are going, and what I need to change/adjust for my students. What does the data say? What needs to be retaught? How can I reach all my students at so many diverse levels in a way that will allow them to show understanding to mastery? So many wheels turning, so many balls to juggle. How can I do it all?

I feel like these are the seasons a tree goes through, all of which are necessary. However, they bring about several changes on the outside of the tree's appearance and not only do these changes impact the tree physically, but the tree also responds in a like manner, becoming stronger, having grown and been through several seasons. The first time you wonder if you will survive, but each year and the changes that come will renew your focus, and you become stronger and more knowledgeable.

The Switch from Title of Teacher to Educator – Strong Branches

Thus begins the movement from just being a teacher to becoming a bonafide educator. You may be asking or saying, what is she talking about? Aren't the two one and the same, just another way of saying a person who works in this field? Well, hopefully after I finish explaining my theory as to why I believe they are indeed two different things, you will be nodding your head in agreement.

Okay, follow me on this compare and contrast…

- Teacher – Qualified, comes to work on time (most days).
- Bonafide Educator – Take the above and add volunteers for various student groups after school, teaching at summer school, and tutoring.
- Teacher—Supports your team and offers help to other colleagues.

- Bonafide Educator – Becomes a team leader and shares ideas, producing innovative ways to accomplish not only their classroom challenges but also collaborating with others.

These are just a couple of ways that I have distinguished one from the other. Of course, this is just my opinion and my perspective/experiences. I would just like to say this is not a scientific fact. So now, this is what I like to refer to as "**Strong Branches.**" It is something to aspire to, and like strong branches on a tree provide support and eventually shade for others, this is what I feel a bonafide educator does for the field of education. Providing that support not only for their students, giving them a safe place to land, etc. but also doing so for their team members and the entire campus community.

Crossroads – Tree Variations

To close this out, I will say I am at the point now that I want to venture out into either another grade level or try another campus or even another district, just to get a new experience. There are so many opportunities within teaching that I know I could never get bored (as I typically do in my life). I am very easily bored, and I will say it's because I have varied interests. I love the fact that I can try something else and get a whole other experience, gaining a new perspective and maintaining my profession. That makes working in this field feel so expansive. And on top of those opportunities, you can also go upward (Assistant Principal, Principal, Superintendent) if you really want to soar in your leadership qualities. It's a vast world! Big enough to come to see where you would fit in and how you can grow and make a real impact on others' lives (including your own).

So, with all of that, why am I now feeling like I am at a crossroads? I am telling myself, as I write this, to understand the process is not always linear. Not with teaching, not with the students learning, and not in life in general, so I want to encourage myself to trust the process and allow it to do its work in and around me. Yet, there is a part of me that says, new year, new decision, new outlook! And, well, I will end here with the thought that I know this profession offers so much. I am willing to put in the work for another branch to grow outside of my grade level or subject area.

I really hope that my tree is bamboo. Do know how they grow? Let me end with another little tidbit of science on that. According to research on the internet, you can find information that speaks to how the Chinese Bamboo grows. It takes a few years underground before you ever see anything, but when it does come up, it can grow several inches per hour, amounting to an average of about three feet per day. They grow extremely tall to about 80-90 feet. Now I say that I am impressed by this because I would love to grow fast so I can be impactful/resourceful for my students immediately; however, that is not to say that there are no flaws or imperfections with this type of tree. I'm just trying to glean from the positives.

I love the world of education, teaching, coaching, protecting, guiding, supporting, sponsoring, instructing, tutelage... there are so many more ways I could describe it, but you get the picture. These are all the things you can be - come join us! Okay, okay, one last quote, I promise. I got this t-shirt from a wonderful PD (Professional Development) recently and I cannot help myself…. "**Those who can't <u>wait to change the world</u>, teach.**" IS THAT YOU???

Megan Gray

Special Education Educator

Megan Gray's journey in education began in 2016. Beyond the classroom, she wears the hat of being a foster parent, extending care to those who need it. She strives to be an advocate for mental health and is dedicated to fostering a supportive environment. Megan's love for literature makes her an avid reader, and she finds solace and joy in quality family time. Through this chapter Megan hopes to encourage her fellow educators to take advantage of the impact teachers have in the lives of youth.

TEACHING FOR BELONGING: A JOURNEY OF PURPOSE AND CONNECTION

By Megan Gray

Just about every year (twice a year, or more realistically, once in August when we are fueled with excitement and anxiety for the year to begin, and again in January after returning from break with the same anxiety, this time with a hint of doubt that we just may not make it another five and half months to the end of the school year), our school principal will ask us to take a moment to think about our "*why*". *Why* are you here? *Why* are you a teacher? *Why* did you choose this path? *Why* did you come back another year? *Why* do you think you have what it takes to fuel a room full of tiny learning minds with education? *Why* do you teach?

Each time I hear the question, I have the same answer. My "why" is simple. For the students.

I am here, *I am* a teacher, *I* chose this path, *I* come back year after year. *I* think I have what it takes to fuel a room full of tiny learning minds with education. *I* teach because of students, because of kids.

I was the type of student who received an assignment that was due weeks later and had it turned in the next day. I was the type of student to read ahead a few chapters so that I would know the answers to questions that would be asked next week. I was the type of student to volunteer to pass out papers and help out students who were having a harder time grasping the skills and wanted to have lunch with the teacher.

However, I was also the type of student to look up information about current trends so I would have things to talk about at recess with my peers. I would reenact conversations with friends the way I wish they had gone with my Fisher-Price little people at home with my door shut after school. Or I'd be the one to eat lunch in the bathroom when I didn't have the same lunch as my one best friend. As a neurodivergent student, I never quite felt a space where I belonged with my peers existed. However, when I finished early, studied ahead, and helped out, I found a safe space with my teachers.

I felt a sense of belonging with my 9th-grade algebra teacher who would let me stay after class to help me master the skill of solving for *x*. I felt a sense of belonging with my 8th-grade journalism teacher when he would use my papers as examples in class. I felt a sense of belonging with my 7th-grade reading teacher who bought me a basket full of new books written by my favorite author and would talk about them with me as I finished reading them. I felt a sense of belonging with my 4th-grade teacher who would take a few minutes to talk about normal life with the class and laugh at some of my silly comments. I felt a sense of belonging with my first and 2nd-grade teachers who took back my one and only conduct mark after I explained why I just *had* to talk out during *silent* work time.

As I got older and the teachers started to fade from being superheroes to adults who led my high school classes, I started to realize that these people who made me feel like I belonged were just humans too. Because amid those teachers who made me feel like I belonged, I had teachers who did the opposite. I encountered a PE coach with a consistently tough demeanor that diminished my enjoyment of elementary PE. Additionally, a history teacher employed "tough love," publicly addressing a low grade with a confrontational approach. Moreover, a school counselor breached my trust by informing my mom about an incident involving me kissing a girl in the hallway, despite me explicitly stating I was not ready to come out to my mom yet. I aged, and teachers got younger, and eventually, they became my peers. Those elementary school students I struggled to talk to in my free time or high school students whom I struggled to sit next to and relate to at lunch became my college classmates and eventually coworkers. There were no teachers to find connection with. I was an adult in the real world, and every other adult was a peer.

I initially went to college with the end goal of being a nurse. I had finished my prerequisite nursing classes and passed the nursing program entry exam at the same point when I took a job as a nurse's aide in a public elementary school.

The nurse's office was attached to the school's self-contained special education class, and I would do tube feedings for a student twice a day. I built a relationship with him and some of the other students and eventually would spend my lunch and other free moments in the classroom. Instant fulfillment. There was a room full of students who would laugh, play, talk, and joke around with their teachers and aides, but would turn into completely different students around their peers. I realized that since now adults were my peers, it meant kids were not. I was no longer trying to find belonging in kids as they were doing this with me instead. The roles were reversed, and I found belonging in the students who found belonging in me.

It took about two weeks into my new job for me to change my career path from nursing to psychology. Two years later, I was taking my first teaching job as a special education teacher in a classroom geared towards teaching neurodivergent students who benefited from structure and social skills.

This next sentence may be a bit controversial, but hang on as I will explain myself. I mean it when I say that *being a teacher is easy.*

It is extremely easy to teach kids specific skills, to build relationships with young little minds. It is extremely easy to be myself around young people and be real with them. It is overwhelmingly difficult at times though to be a peer to other teachers and adults. Being a teacher to students is why I come back every year. It is the data, numbers, angry parents, frustrating coworkers, paperwork, lesson plans, bulletin boards, checklists, grading, and dreadful arrival and dismissal duties that make me question how much it is worth coming back to every year. I speak for most teachers when I say if all I had to do was come in and teach lessons to students paired with a conference period and lunch, I would come back every morning with significantly less stress and anxiety about what each day may bring.

As I have said, it is my peers that make my life a little more difficult to navigate. Living life as a neurodivergent person, it has rung true in nearly every setting. However, when I pull a group of students to provide whatever service I am in charge of providing that year, I find that there are young, neurodivergent minds out there who are longing for the same sense of security that I am (honestly, that we all are).

Almost immediately at the start of my teaching journey, I learned that my job as a teacher is to do more than just teach. In order to teach, I have to have a room full of students who listen to me. In order to have a room full of students who listen to me, I have to have a room full of students who respect me. In order to have a room full of students who respect me, I have to have a room full of students who know me. In order to have that, I must take the time to get to know *them*. With full confidence, I can tell you that it is the journey of getting to know students that makes being a teacher so rewarding for me.

In one memorable instance, I noticed a student consistently sitting alone during recess, seemingly isolated from their peers. Determined to foster a sense of belonging, I approached the student and struck up a conversation. Over time, I discovered their passion for drawing but reluctance to share their art due to fear of judgment. Through empathetic conversations and encouragement, I created a safe space for them to express themselves. Gradually, the student started sharing their artwork with classmates, and a noticeable transformation occurred as they gained confidence, formed new connections, and found a supportive community within the school. In a more challenging situation, a student-directed hurtful slurs toward me, creating a tense atmosphere. Rather than responding with anger, I chose to approach the student with empathy. I initiated a private conversation to understand their perspective and discovered the underlying struggles they were facing. By expressing genuine concern and offering support, a shift occurred. The student, initially defensive, eventually opened up about their difficulties. Over time, our relationship transformed, and they not only ceased using slurs but also became more receptive to guidance and positive interactions, demonstrating the transformative power of compassion in fostering understanding and change. In reflecting on these experiences, it becomes evident that empathy has the transformative power to bridge gaps and cultivate positive change. Whether it's fostering a sense of belonging through encouragement or diffusing hostility with compassionate understanding, these anecdotes underscore the impact that empathetic connections can have on students, shaping not only their individual growth but also contributing to the overall, positive atmosphere within the educational environment.

When I am able to become the teacher that I once needed when I was in school, then I will be able to teach students reading and social skills simultaneously and hopefully make a difference deeper than I would as just their fourth-grade dyslexia teacher.

I believe that as teachers our job is to meet students where they are educationally, yes, but also emotionally and socially. A student will not learn from us if they do not want to; we have to encourage students to want to learn.

As a neurodivergent individual, I faced the ongoing challenge of understanding and navigating the social intricacies of the education system. Moments of self-discovery often revolved around finding coping mechanisms for sensory sensitivities and dealing with the pressure to conform to conventional learning styles. I vividly recall instances where I felt overwhelmed in crowded classrooms or struggled to express myself verbally, leading to a sense of isolation. However, through these challenges, I discovered unique strengths such as a heightened ability to focus on details and a deep passion for certain subjects. Embracing my neurodivergence became a journey of self-acceptance, allowing me to bring a valuable perspective to both my personal experiences and my interactions within the educational realm. By recognizing the transformative power of self-acceptance and understanding the impact it had on my own educational journey, I have become fueled by a passionate commitment to guide and support students in their pursuit of self-discovery by providing them with the tools and encouragement to embrace their individual strengths and navigate the educational landscape with confidence.

I am a teacher because I want to offer students who are like me the acceptance that I longed for. I want to ensure that they are being heard, understood, seen, and taken care of beyond their academic needs. So each year, when I am asked to think of my "*why*," I think of elementary school me and of those teachers who gave me a sense of security (and also those who didn't). I am a good teacher. I know I am. I am good at making my students feel loved. I am good at helping my students learn. I am good at providing a safe space for little brains, and I know this because I feel it too. I learn and feel love and safety often. I am a teacher because it's the small choices in the moment of offering love to little minds that are enough to change a student's day, year, or life.

I teach for the kids. Even when deadlines make my job difficult or adults run my patience thin, I remind myself to separate that from the kids. They deserve belonging and love every day because I deserve the same.

Denise Mustin

Founder of Instructional Impact, LLC

https://www.linkedin.com/in/denise-mustin-9b62bb239
https://www.facebook.com/denise.mustin.5
https://twitter.com/DeniseMustin

Denise Mustin has served for 31 years in public education and continues to give her all to the teachers, students, and parents she works with on a daily basis. She didn't always want to be an educator and fought it for a little bit, but God had other plans and made sure she ended up walking in her purpose as an educator. She continued in her own education to receive her master's and doctoral degrees in education. She has seen the good, the bad, the ugly, but mostly the GREAT things that go on behind the schoolhouse doors and hopes to share those amazing stories with everyone that wants to listen.

HIS NAME IS JAMES

By Denise Mustin

As I was preparing for my third year of teaching, my first year as a fourth grade teacher, I looked around the empty classroom and began making plans for exactly how I wanted my classroom setup. I arranged the desks in so many different ways that I became dizzy but eventually settled on arranging them in groups of four. I loved having students work in collaborative groups, and this arrangement made it more efficient. I walked in circles for a bit around the room, wondering about what students I would have that year, and reflected on all the things I was going to be able to teach. I finally focused on the next task and was hanging a banner up that had my favorite saying on it - "You are the author of your own life story!" - when another teacher stopped by my room. She asked me if I had received my class roster for the year yet. I nodded yes and told her that it was on my desk, but that I hadn't looked at it yet. She was a veteran teacher, a leader on campus, and I looked to her as a mentor even though she could be a little bossy.

She picked up my roster and scanned it quickly, making noises of affirmation, gave a few smiles with expressive eyebrows, and then she suddenly stopped and came over to me and said, "Oh no! You got him!" She continued quickly, spouting off, "We all wondered who would be the lucky one. I'm so sorry. You are going to have a bad year. His teacher this past year couldn't do anything with him in the room. Good luck!" She left me staring at her, wondering who in the world she was talking about. It wasn't very long before I was getting condolences everywhere I went across the campus. I started to get a little worried about having this student in my classroom. I went to question my principal about the student and asked him if he thought that I would be the best teacher for a student with his reputation considering I only had two years of teaching experience.

He responded very simply, "You are the exact teacher he needs." I wasn't sure what that meant at the time, but knew there wasn't much I could do about the situation. I decided to ignore all further comments from my peers and continue preparing for the school year like any other.

The first day of school came, and I was greeting each new student and their parents as they entered the classroom. I had them sit at the seats I had prepared for them with a little welcome gift and an activity to work on while I greeted the other students. The tardy bell rang and I was about to close the door when I heard feet running down the hall and a voice saying, "I'm here, I'm here!" Before I could react, the door I was closing was pushed frantically open, and there stood this husky boy with bright red hair sticking up all over in strange ways, big blue eyes staring at me through big, rimmed glasses; as he wiped snot off his nose with his shirt collar. I looked around the door to see if any parents were behind him, but there was no one there. "I'm Junior," he said quickly, and his eyes began darting around the room.

I could hear sighs and groans behind me and very clearly heard one boisterous student say, "Oh no, not him!" Junior seemed to ignore it. I gave the "teacher look" to the vocal student and slowly showed Junior his assigned seat. A student in that group said, "Ms. Teacher, he usually sits at a desk all by himself."

I just smiled and said, "Well this is a new year and you guys are big 4th graders now, so we are going to all learn to work together." As soon as those words came out of my mouth, Junior fell completely backward in his chair, landing on the floor with a thud and papers flying everywhere. He looked up at me through his crooked classes and said, "I'm ok!"

That first day was a blur; I mean most first days of school are, but this one was different. I went home exhausted and doubted my abilities to teach this hurricane who called himself Junior.

The next day wasn't much better. Junior required a lot of space. He didn't seem to understand how his movements affected everyone else around him. To this day, I have never had a student who could make one book, one piece of paper, and one pencil take up the space of two desks and have a little whirlwind behind him constantly like a character in the Peanuts cartoon. Those first few weeks of school consisted of me refereeing between Junior and every other student in class. It was like a recording playing all day long: "He is touching me," "He is staring at me," "His stuff is on my desk," "He is making faces at me," "He won't stop talking," "He is pushing," "He cut in line," "He tore the book," "He kicked me," "He is picking his boogers." The complaints went on and on.

About a month into school, Junior went to the restroom. When he hadn't returned in a few minutes, I went to look for him. I could hear a faint voice saying, "Help me! Help me, please," but I didn't see anyone in the hallway. The library was next to the bathroom and outside of the library was a little red schoolhouse book return. I looked in the book slot and saw those big blue eyes staring back at me. It was Junior; he had found a way to open the door, crawl in the book drop, and close the door behind him, which was locked. I was able to get the key and rescue him, after which he thanked me with a big bear hug that left snot on my dress.

Up to this point, I had not been able to get his parents to come to an in-person conference with me, but when I called them this time, I insisted we had to meet soon. They finally agreed to come. When Junior's mom walked in, I recognized her immediately. They had the same red hair sticking out in all directions, big blue eyes peering out of big-rimmed glasses, and freckles. His dad was smaller in stature and had brown hair that was brushed slick back and greasy. His mom blurted out in a long-winded breath, "So what did Junior do now? I guess you want him thrown out of your class too, huh? He is always causing problems. His dad drives a truck and is never home, and well, we don't know what to do with him either!" She almost fell back in the chair herself when she sat down quickly. The dad slumped back in the chair next to her. She didn't even flinch. "So, tell us what he did now so we can take him home and beat him."

I paused for a moment, taking in their presence, and immediately understood why Junior was the way he was. I also immediately understood why they didn't think he had any real behavior problems. He was only behaving just like his parents, and it was clear the entire family probably had some form of undiagnosed ADHD and lacked self-regulation and emotional control skills. Of course, not having a medical degree, I couldn't say what I was thinking. I took a deep breath and took an entirely different approach. I smiled and said, "I'm actually enjoying having Junior in my class this year. He is full of energy and has caused some trouble, but he is really smart. My goal is to help him learn how to control himself so he can show the world how intelligent he is." They both sat up in their chairs and just stared at me. I took another breath and shared with them a few examples of work where Junior had demonstrated his gifted thinking. Again, they just stared.

Finally, the dad asked, "You think my son is smart?" I was able to explain that I did indeed think he was smart, but that his behavior was so extreme it was stopping him from learning as well as interfering with the learning of his classmates. I told them I planned to work with him to change his behaviors, but I needed their help with reinforcement of those behaviors at home. They looked at each other and then at me, and I knew they didn't know how to do that. I ended the meeting by thanking them for coming in to meet with me and saying that I would be in touch with them again soon. They asked if he was suspended, and I told them no, that being locked in the box was a lesson enough. They left without another word. I couldn't tell what they were thinking, but I knew nothing was going to change quickly to help Junior.

The next day, Junior came running down the hall late. His hair was sticking up all over the place again. His hair was always an indication to me of what his day was going to be like. If it was somewhat brushed, it wouldn't be too bad, but if it was sticking up all over, it was going to be a rough day. He slid into the classroom like a baseball player sliding into home base. His backpack went flying, knocking a classmate down. "Guess what, Miss? My dad says he thinks you are too nice." Then he went and sat at his self-selected personal desk. I had no idea what that meant or what to say, so I just welcomed him to class and asked him to try entering the class the correct way. To my surprise, he did and did it correctly, and even apologized to the student who was hit by his flying backpack.

Later that same day, when I was picking up my class from lunch, another teacher came to tell me again how bad Junior (who they nicknamed Dennis the Menace); had been at lunch and how they didn't know how I put up with him all day. Some days, I didn't know either. I was constantly researching ways to help him control himself. I went home several nights crying and wondering how I could help him while keeping all the other students in the classroom safe and learning.

Day after day, the school year continued the same way. Junior would show up late, move around the room like a bull in a China cabinet, annoy his classmates with his constant moving and sarcastic remarks, blurt out anything that popped into his head, and pick a fight with any student who dared to say anything to him he didn't like. And day after day, I worked with him on controlling his actions, completing his work, and intervening to keep him out of trouble with others while trying to teach the rest of my students.

Then, at our class Christmas party which he was barely able to attend, he made it across the room and punched another student in the nose before I could blink. The parents there were shocked, and I was stunned and embarrassed as I took Junior's hand and walked him to the hallway, only stopping to call the front office for help. Junior immediately began crying hard, and I couldn't understand what he was trying to tell me. He went to the office while the other student was taken care of by the nurse, and I shakily finished the Christmas party for the other students and reassured parents that this would never happen again. Once all the parents left, I was able to go to the office to meet with Junior. It was here that I learned that the reason Junior hit the other students was because that student had made fun of Junior's gift for the gift exchange and told him nobody would want it because he was so gross.

What that student didn't understand was that Junior's family didn't have money to participate. What I didn't know was that Junior selected a book that I had given him early in the year to give away. A book he cherished but was willing to give away in order to participate. The only good thing that came of the incident was that I was able to meet with his mom in person again. This time I was a little more direct with her. I explained that Junior had a lot of potential but that he was extremely impulsive, lacked emotional control, and truly seemed to not be able to control himself even on "good" days. This time, instead of making excuses, the mom began to cry and explained that I had just described her and her entire life. She asked what she could do to help Junior have a better chance than she did. I recommended that she take Junior to his pediatrician and explain the concerns. She said she would.

In January, Junior came barreling in, nothing different. I don't know what I thought would happen; I guess I wanted a miracle. Mid-January was the time to have the "possibility of failing" meeting with parents of students who did not have passing grades. When Junior's parents came in, the dad was defensive and explained that I should be more concerned about teaching Junior than getting him on medicine. I was confused as I had never said those words. The mom said that she had taken Junior to the doctor and that he mentioned ADHD and medication. The dad said, "My son don't need no medicine!" and left the room. The mom looked at me with a pleading look and then left as well. I knew then that the only help Junior was going to get would be from me, so I vowed to learn everything I could about helping students with ADHD. I put many accommodations in place. Some helped, some didn't, but life in the classroom with Junior remained tough.

As the Valentine's party approached, I wondered if Junior should be allowed to participate in the party at all. I didn't want a Christmas repeat. I called his mom to see if she would be able to attend the party with him. Once again, she started crying and explained she had just lost her job, again. She said she could come to the party but couldn't afford to get him Valentine's cards. I told her I had extra, she just needed to come and spend time with her son.

While I had been researching ADHD, I learned how it affected adults. One effect of adults with undiagnosed ADHD was that they often would bounce from job to job (or get fired frequently.) I asked the mom to meet with me after the party and asked for an update on where they were at with Junior and his doctor. She said that her husband refused to believe Junior had ADHD and refused medication for him. She asked if I had anything that could convince him. I explained that I was not a medical professional or his parents but that I had found some pamphlets regarding the effects of ADHD on adults as well as one for students that included characteristic checklists. I explained that she could have them to read.

Junior was Junior until Spring Break. When we returned from Spring Break, Junior's face was clean, his hair brushed, and he walked - yes walked - into class. I just thought maybe he was going to have a good day, but the next day was the same, and he actually completed all his work. At the end of the week, I realized that I hadn't had to redirect Junior all week. I called his mom to brag about him. Again, she began to cry and said, "It's working! It is working for both of us!" She explained that she could not let Junior grow up the way she had and have the life she has had so far and that she and he were both diagnosed with ADHD and now on medication. I told her that I had noticed a remarkable difference and would continue to monitor him for her. I also told her that nominations for the Gifted and Talented Program were being accepted and that I was going to nominate him for the GT program. I could hear her smile through the phone.

Junior qualified for GT by receiving one of the highest scores ever scored. He began to excel in academics, and I could even read his handwriting. As May approached, I began to get mixed emotions about the school year ending. Despite being a challenge, this class had really grown on me, especially Junior. On the last day of school, he came running into the class with a big smile on his face and practically threw a gift bag at me. Inside was a hodgepodge of items that he must have found around his home - a silk flower, a used lipstick, a toy ring. I smiled, knowing he was giving me what he could because he wanted to give me something, but then I read the card. In his now neat handwriting, the card read, "Thank you for believing in me. I love you!" and it was signed "James!" I called him over and gave him a big hug and asked why he signed the card James instead of Junior. His blue eyes were bright and big as he smiled and said, "Because I'm never going to act like Junior again. My name is James!"

I followed up with James when he was graduating high school. He had some ups and downs in his school career, but he graduated with honors and was headed to college on an academic scholarship to study architecture and/or engineering. His goal was to be a theme park designer. A small tear rolled down my cheek as they announced his name as "James" as he walked across the stage to receive his diploma.

It was at that moment that I realized how, in many ways, our students are more of a hero to us than we are to them. James' mom called me a hero at his graduation, but all I did was love and support him through a rough time in his education career and dare to not give up on him or his parents. He was the one who had to accept his challenges and make the decision to work hard to make the changes he needed to be successful and not give up on himself.

I share this story in hopes of inspiring all teachers who have a "Junior" in their classroom. With all the pressures of accountability and required mandates and expectations, students' real needs can become lost. Many educators can share their burnout and frustrations to the point that they negatively influence the way they and other educators begin to think about their calling to be teachers. The day-to-day tasks can be hard and at times discouraging. I had to experience the entire year to know if anything I did made a difference or not. Thirty years later, I have many stories like this one, and the good times definitely outweigh the tough times. I encourage you, whether you are in your first year or thirtieth year of teaching, to always remember that you are "the right teacher at the right time," and with patience, grit, and love, you can become their hero and they can become yours.

Spread Our Message!

The Heroes in Our Classrooms

With Cheri Dixon Consulting, LLC

Cheri Dixon Consulting, LLC was formed in June of 2023, after Cheri left her career of 28 years in public education. Cheri served as a teacher and school administrator and believes in the power of teachers! *The Heroes in Our Classrooms* is her way to share stories from educators that had an impact on her own educational journey, with hope that these stories will inspire anyone thinking of joining the teaching profession, needing a little extra boost as he/she navigates the world of public education, or just as an enjoyable read! May you laugh and cry, but most importantly, remember why you said yes to the most impactful profession out there!

Looking to build your own teaching skills?

Cheri Dixon Consulting offers a variety of supports for teachers and administrators who are in the world of education! I would love to connect with you and see how I can support you as you build your skills and become the best educator you can be!

Visit my website and join From Rookie to Rockstar,
where you can get support as you navigate your way through your
rookie years as a teacher!

https://teachersthatsparkleorg.wordpress.com

Are you an aspiring or current school leader and want the right
cheerleader by your side so you can level up your skills and take your
organization from average to amazing? Email me and let's schedule a
call to discuss your journey and how we can work together to get you
on your path to unimaginable success!

cheri@cheridixonconsulting.com

Visit cheridixonconsulting.com to see how YOU can build a life you
love, fulfilling all your goals and dreams personally and professionally!

Have you checked out the *Strong: Inside and Out Podcast?*

Find me on Apple and Spotify Podcasts!

Join me on my journey in the world of media!

Not only can you catch my talk show, *Confident, Courageous and Clear with Cheri*, but you can find my first documentary, *Somewhere on the Spectrum: Navigating the World of Autism*!

Visit <u>Fenix TV</u> for details!

www.ingramcontent.com/pod-product-compliance
Lightning Source LLC
Chambersburg PA
CBHW070937120626
46546CB00004B/1443